Common Word Far

Vocabulary:

hop

mop

pop

top

drop

flop

plop

stop

Directions:

Page 1: Cut apart the word cards on the inside back cover and review the __op vocabulary. To extend, the child can draw pictures on corresponding cards and play a matching memory game.

Pages 2-5: Child writes the vocabulary words on the stop signs three times each and colors them. If you have access to a duplicating machine, the stop signs can be copied, cut out, and stapled together to make a book.

Page 6: Child writes the words in alphabetical order onto the stop signs. Child can then color the picture.

Page 7: Child reads the rebus sentences and writes the missing words in the blanks.

Write each word three times. Color the stop signs.

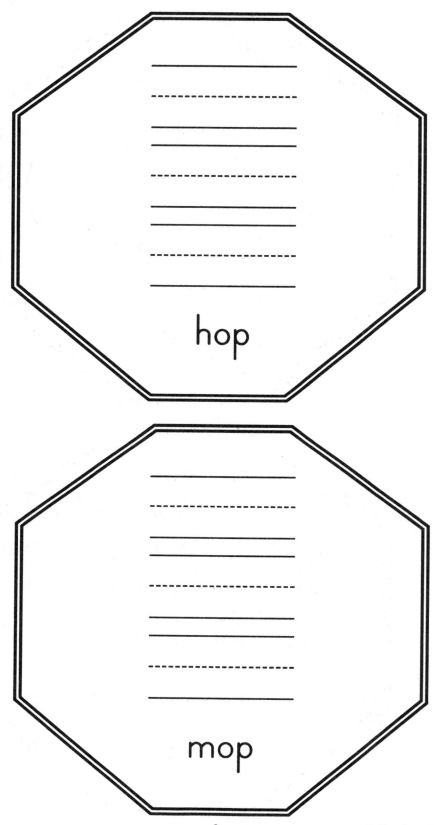

hop

mop

Write each word three times. Color the stop signs.

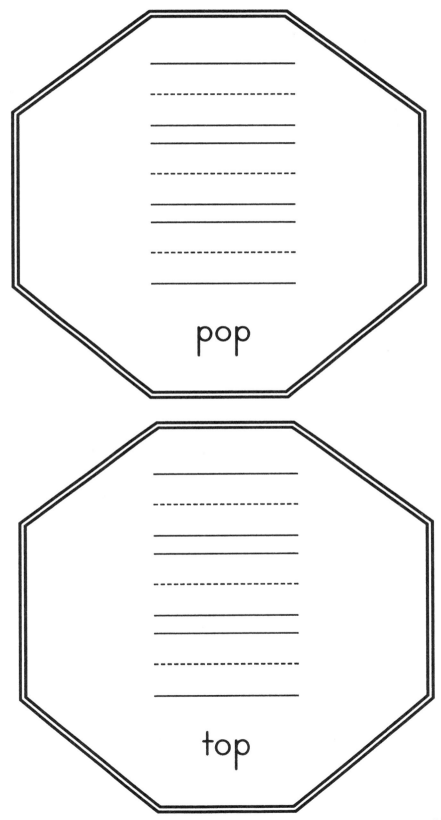

pop

top

Write each word three times. Color the stop signs.

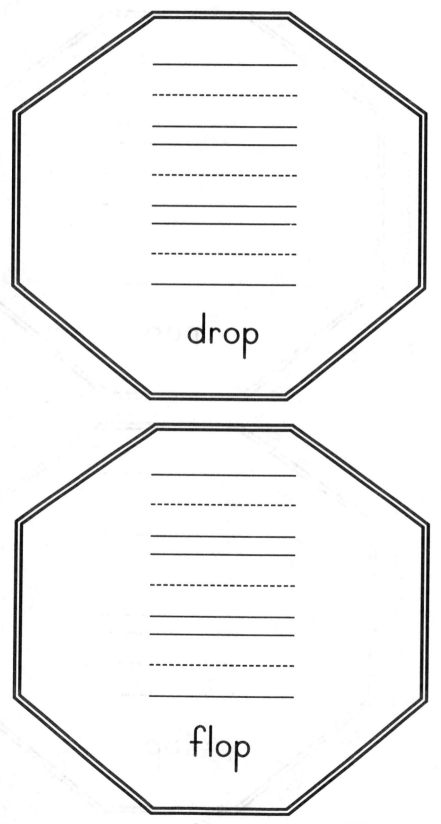

drop

flop

Write each word three times. Color the stop signs.

plop

stop

Write the words in ABC order next to
the correct numeral along the road.

abcdefghijklmnopqrstuvwxyz

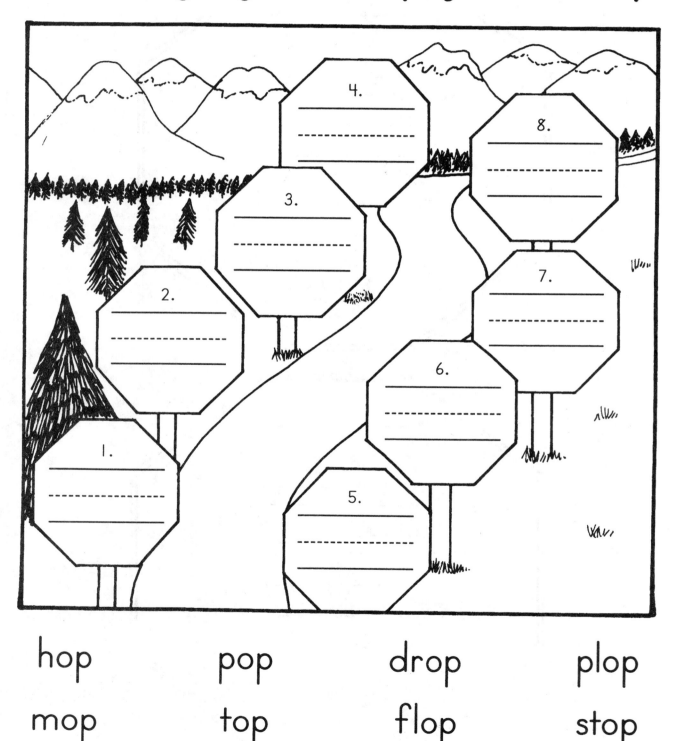

hop   pop   drop   plop

mop   top   flop   stop

Read the sentences. Write the missing words on the lines.

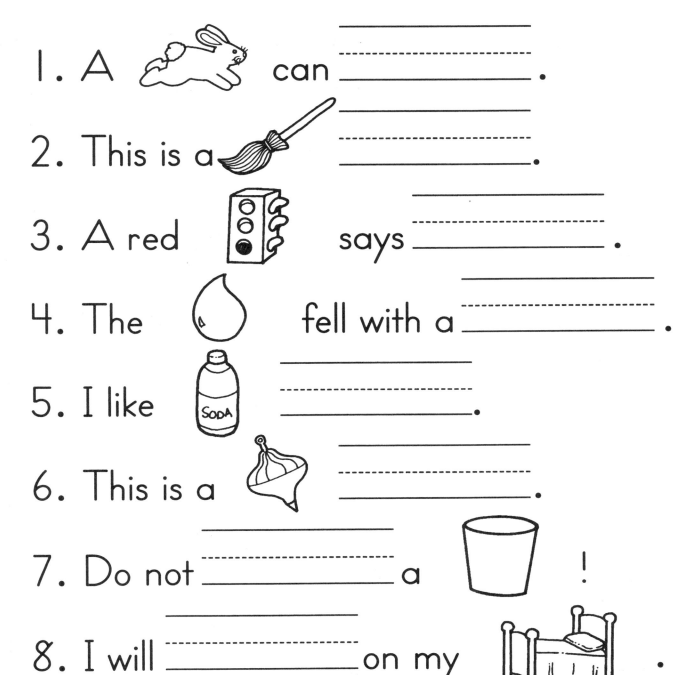

1. A 🐇 can _____.

2. This is a 🧹 _____.

3. A red 🚦 says _____.

4. The 💧 fell with a _____.

5. I like SODA _____.

6. This is a 🌀 _____.

7. Do not _____ a 🪣 !

8. I will _____ on my 🛏 .

hop	pop	mop	stop
plop	drop	top	flop

Common Word Family __ot

Vocabulary:

dot

got

hot

lot

not

pot

spot

trot

Directions:

Page 8: Cut apart the word cards on the inside back cover and review the __ot vocabulary. To extend, the child can draw pictures on corresponding cards and play a matching memory game.

Pages 9-10: Child writes the vocabulary words on the pots three times each and colors them. If you have access to a duplicating machine, the pots can be copied, cut out, and stapled together to make a book.

Page 11: Child cuts out the word boxes and glues them in alphabetical order in the bubbles. Child can then color the picture.

Page 13: Child circles the vocabulary words in the word search. They can be found across or down. Child can then color the picture.

Page 14: Child colors the rhyming __ot words green and the other words yellow to see a flower pot.

Page 15: Child changes one letter in each word to make __ot words.

Write each word three times. Color the pots.

dot

hot

got

lot

Write each word three times. Color the pots.

not

pot

spot

trot

Cut out the word boxes. Glue them in ABC order in the bubbles. Color the picture.

a b c d e f g h i j k l m n o p q r s t u v w x y z

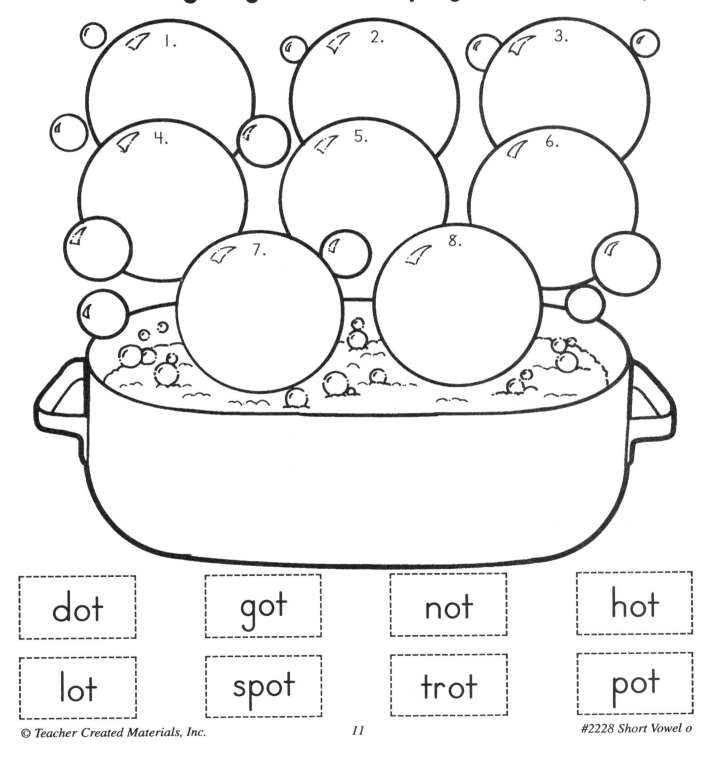

| dot | got | not | hot |
| lot | spot | trot | pot |

12

Circle the words in the puzzle. Color the picture.

dot hot not spot
got lot pot trot

t e n l e t d t d

r o n o t a i i o

o p o t s r h p t

t a n r p n o p s

t o t a o p t o o

s g o t t u n t t

h a t e a t e n o

Color the spaces with the rhyming **ot** words green. Color the other spaces yellow. What do you see?

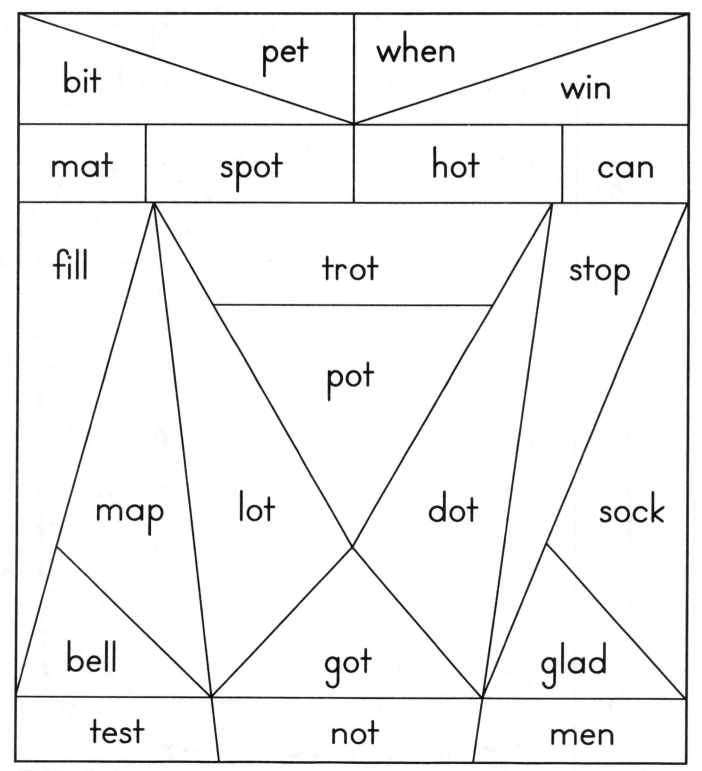

bit	pet	when	win
mat	spot	hot	can
fill	trot		stop
	pot		
map	lot	dot	sock
bell	got		glad
test	not		men

Change one letter in each word to make an **ot** word. Write the new words.

1. hat _____

2. let _____

3. pit _____

4. net _____

5. get _____

6. spat _____

got   lot   pot
hot   not   spot

Common Word Family __ock

Vocabulary:

dock

lock

rock

sock

block

clock

knock

shock

Directions:

Page 16: Cut apart the word cards on the inside back cover and review the __ock vocabulary. To extend, the child can draw pictures on corresponding cards and play a matching memory game.

Pages 17-20: Child writes the vocabulary words on the socks three times each and colors them. If you have access to a duplicating machine, the socks can be copied, cut out, and stapled together to make a book.

Page 21: Child colors and cuts out the socks and glues them in alphabetical order on the clothesline.

Page 23: Child fills in the crossword blocks with the correct vocabulary words.

Page 24: Child circles the vocabulary words in the word search. They can be found across or down. Child can then color the picture.

Write each word three times. Color the sock.

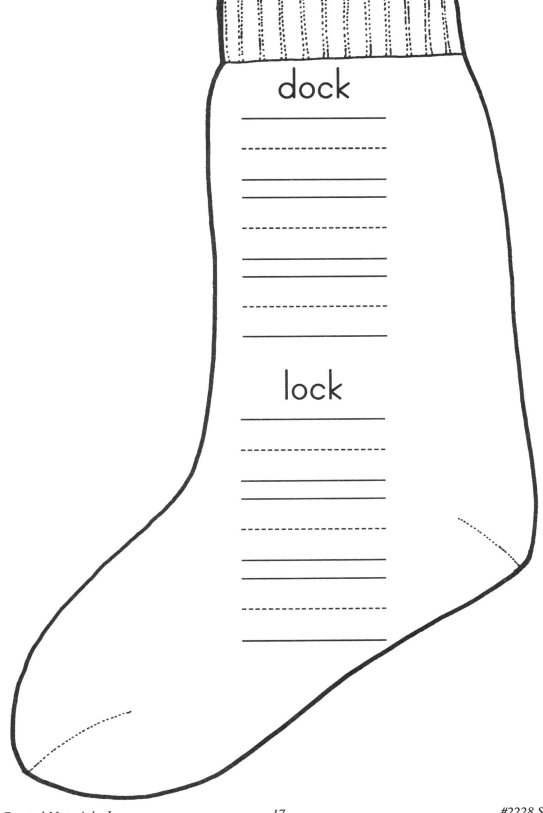

dock

lock

Write each word three times. Color the sock.

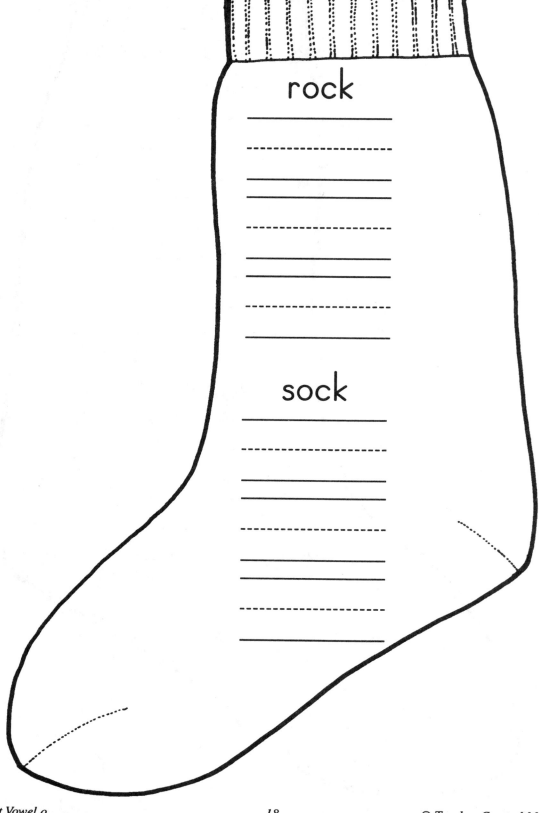

rock

sock

Write each word three times. Color the sock.

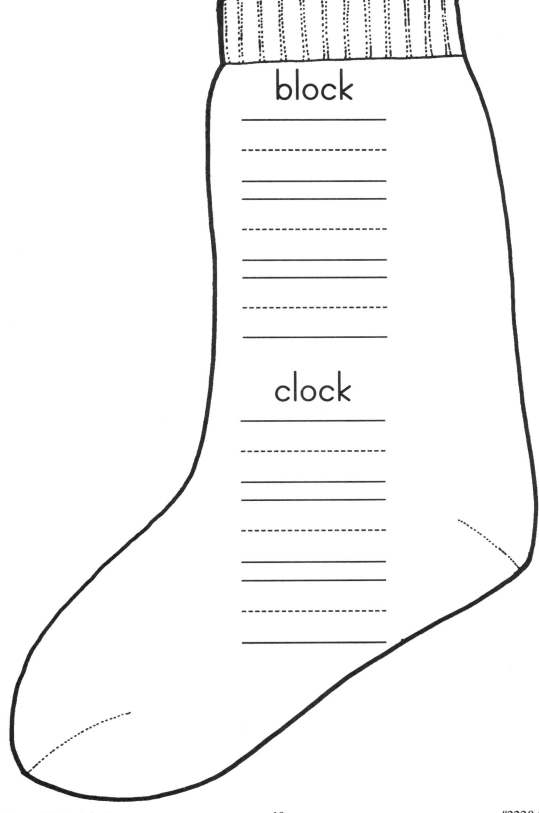

block

clock

Write each word three times. Color the sock.

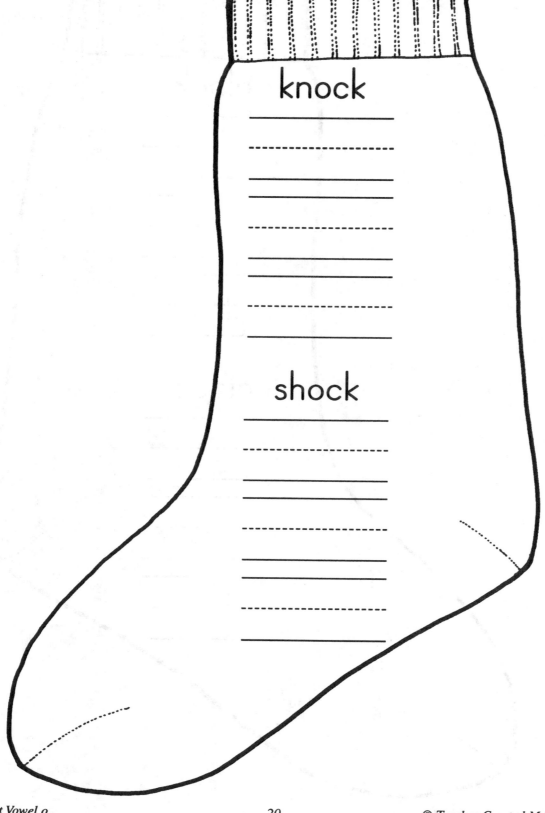

knock

shock

Color the socks and the clothesline. Cut out the socks and glue them in ABC order to the clothesline.

a b c d e f g h i j k l m n o p q r s t u v w x y z

1 2 3 4 5 6 7 8

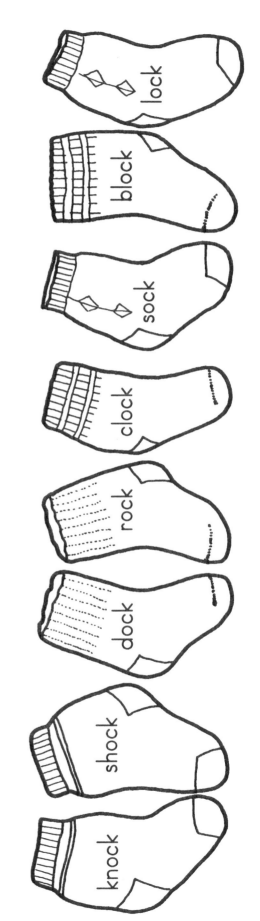

lock

block

sock

clock

rock

dock

shock

knock

22

Fill in the crossword blocks with the correct words.

dock knock lock block
shock rock clock sock

1. ⬚⬚⬚⬚⬚

2. ⬚⬚⬚⬚⬚⬚

3. ⬚⬚⬚⬚

4. ⬚⬚⬚⬚⬚⬚

5. ⬚⬚⬚⬚⬚

6. ⬚⬚⬚⬚⬚⬚

7. ⬚⬚⬚⬚

8. ⬚⬚⬚⬚⬚⬚

Circle the words in the puzzle. Color the picture.

dock

lock

rock

sock

block

clock

knock

shock

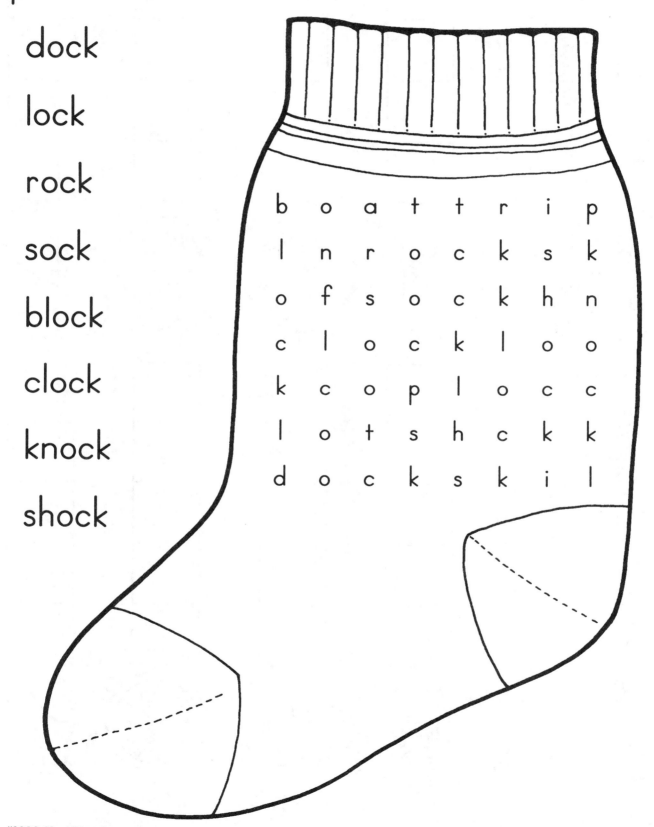

```
b  o  a  t  t  r  i  p
l  n  r  o  c  k  s  k
o  f  s  o  c  k  h  n
c  l  o  c  k  l  o  o
k  c  o  p  l  o  c  c
l  o  t  s  h  c  k  k
d  o  c  k  s  k  i  l
```

Common Word Family __og

Vocabulary:

bog

cog

dog

fog

hog

jog

log

frog

Directions:

Page 25: Cut apart the word cards on the inside back cover and review the __og vocabulary. To extend, the child can draw pictures on corresponding cards and play a matching memory game.

Pages 26-27: Child writes the vocabulary words on the frogs three times each and colors them. If you have access to a duplicating machine, the frogs can be copied, cut out, and stapled together to make a book.

Page 28: Child writes the words in alphabetical order on the frog's spots. Child can then color the picture.

Page 29: Child colors the rhyming __og frogs green. Child can then read the rhyming words.

Page 30: Child circles the vocabulary words in the word search. They can be found across or down. Child can then color the picture.

Write each word three times. Color the frogs.

bog

cog

dog

fog

Write each word three times. Color the frogs.

hog

jog

log

frog

Write the words in ABC order on the frog's spots. Color the frog.

abcdefghijklmnopqrstuvwxyz

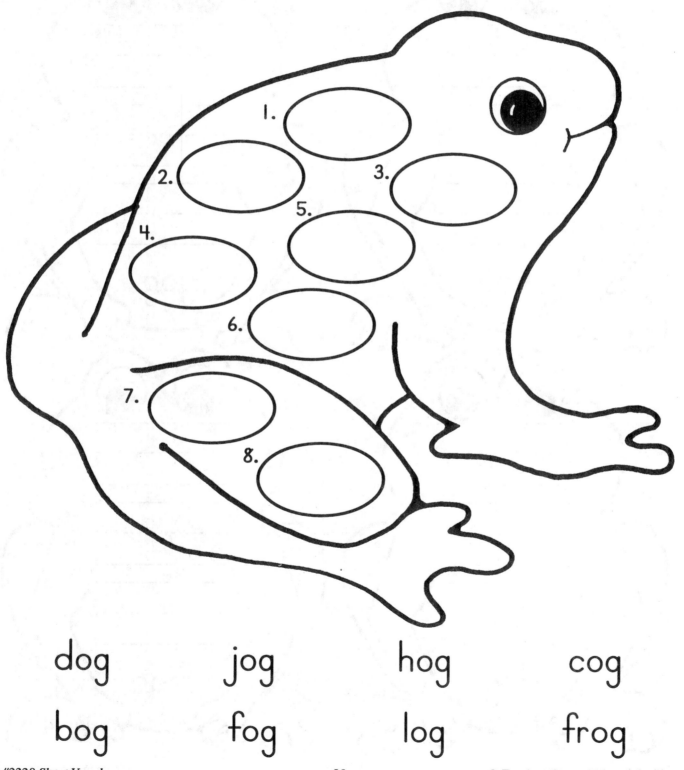

dog   jog   hog   cog

bog   fog   log   frog

Color the rhyming **og** frogs green. Read the rhyming words.

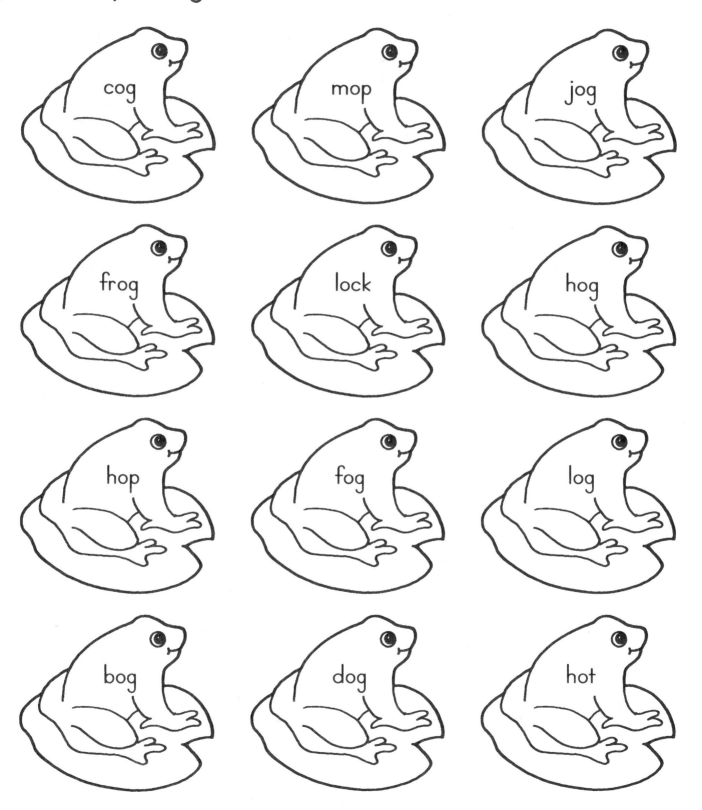

cog

mop

jog

frog

lock

hog

hop

fog

log

bog

dog

hot

Circle the words in the puzzle. Color the picture.

b	o	g	e	g	j	o	t
a	n	a	m	e	o	c	e
g	p	h	o	t	g	z	c
o	g	o	t	e	t	o	o
s	a	g	n	o	f	g	g
f	o	g	a	p	o	o	o
g	l	o	c	t	r	l	m
f	r	o	g	e	g	o	s
d	o	g	o	w	g	g	o

bog   dog   hog   log
cog   fog   jog   frog

Write the words in the correct word family.

not	shock	dot	spot	hop	plop	block	pot
frog	fog	mop	lock	cog	jog	flop	dock
hot	rock	drop	log	got	dog	pop	lot
sock	hog	bog	knock	top	stop	clock	trot

___op

___ot

___ock

___og

Finish each word with **op** or **ot**. Color the pictures.

tr _____

st _____

h _____

p _____

t _____

h _____

sp _____

m _____

Finish each word with **ock** or **og**. Color the pictures.

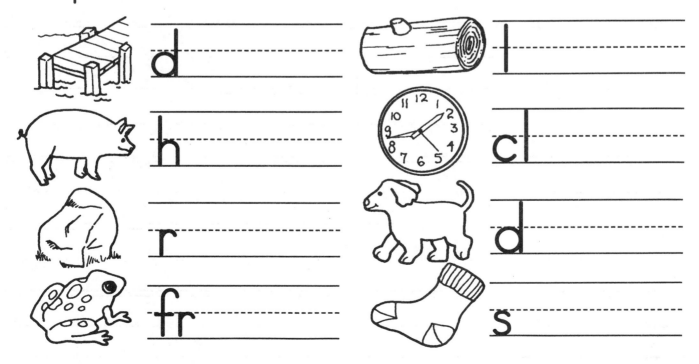

d _____

h _____

r _____

fr _____

l _____

c _____

d _____

s _____